# Found Poems: the blood and bone remember

Patricia A. Bow

ISBN 978-0-9937857-9-5

Published by Patricia Bow Inc

www.execulink.com/~thebows/patricia.htm

Distributed by Lulu Press

www.lulu.com

# Contents:

## Special occasion poems



## New found poems from her journals



## Poems from a 3.5" disc

## Special occasion poems

Winter Poems: written for Eric with love
By Patricia Anne Bow Christmas 1969

Bright balls in boxes,
Shining rolls of paper foil,
Cakes packed up on shelves,

Wait like bridesmaids, while
The tree, shining and fragrant,
Waits the wedding night.

Bare branches tangle
By the December window
To call you to me,
I'll send a squirrel leaping
All the way from tree to tree.

Pillowed this morning,
Daydreams echo all my nights.
I reach out, but know
You're up and gone, dark tiger,
Satin-skinned and almond-eyed.

Saturday morning:
To fill empty streets, the frost
Amplifies footsteps.

Disturbed by the wind,
To and fro above bare trees
Swoops the pigeon flock.

Dusk falls, Prussian blue:
The snow is phosphorescent.
The north wind whistles
Through the Tower. You and I,
Fighting the cold, head for home.

First snow came today:
We look back and see our tracks
Printed side by side.

Alone, my feet are
Always running back to you
On the path of dreams.
Better is one glimpse of you
In all your reality.

1

Snow falls in ambush on
The fir tree, the holly tree.
By her dark circle
Catch me, kiss my snowy face,
Celebrate the holly tree.

2

Trees are blue with lights –
The fir trees, the holly trees –
Holly silver-clad.
Kiss me in the sparkling night,
Close beside the holly tree.

3

Dark and green her heart –
The fir tree, the holly tree –
In Magician's robes,
Casting out her scented spell.
Dance before the holly tree!

In these empty rooms,
Sounds from outside the
windows
Approach like thieves

You rose in the dark
To stop the tap; returning,
Stumbled on the trunk.

Winter roads at night,
When two walk hand in hand, are
Gay as spring sunshine.

The husband absent:
Birds chirp in the silent house
While the wife listens.

All seasons flowing:
This snow, those trees, are altered
From last winter's scene.
Only my soul, transformed, is
Changed by love beyond all change.

A valentine Sonnet to E____
By Patricia A. Bow (1970)

Beside the roses in this red bouquet
Accept the thoughts of flowers I could not buy
Sprays of mezereum to please you by,
Peach blossoms, cedar leaves, that try to say
Why crocuses mean much to me today.
Rampant amongst the others, stretching high.
The rose and myrtle twine in one great sigh,
Now serious, now bending down to play.
Humble but constant, bay leaves down below
Express in fragrance what cannot be said.
Eager and bright, the coxcomb flowers grow
And bring the vital question to a head:
Just answer yes, and give me mistletoe;
Then shall the roses bloom forever red.

ERIC by Patricia A. Bow
February 14, 1970

In the country of my heart
One name is the key to all things.
In my heart's society
Only one name is worth dropping
The seasons say it over
            In their turn,
Even the rain
Drops your name.

My darling Eric (1970?)

Golden lights
In silver trees,
Velvet nights,
Winds that freeze:

Bell and candle,
Fur and feather,
Good friends
Laugh together,
All this is Christmas weather.

Sharing wonders
Old and new'
Sacred time
Alone with you:
Christmas is
This, too.

[Always your most loving wife,
Pat.]

TO
ERIC
21 JUNE 1970

You love me royally, as I love you,
seated together in our garden Kingdom,
keeping up our silent conversation,
clothed in robes of joy of every hue.
For us, our royal love has had no parallel:
It rooted, grew, and like a miracle
spread to the garden where in now we sit,
Clothed in the fragrance of God in it.

And this long miracle is to discover
the inmost me and you,
to nurse no longing for another,
to forge the soul and its desire together
gently, openly and forever.

Nothing grows but common flowers
outside our Kingdom's wall.
Here alone the magic lies.
We ask nothing; we have all.

In 1982 Christmas Card

*Christmas scene of cottage covered in snow – warm glow coming from windows*

Dear Eric,

I chose this card for its blank inside
As much as for its pictured cover:
Meaning to fill it with verses I'd
Dedicate to my own true lover.

But then I saw, the picture told
The tale in full: that's me and you
(and not to leave out you-know-who)
Snug behind those panes of gold,
Beside the fire, out of the cold.
So I decided: no verse would do.

For poems are made by fools like me,
But only God can make a thee.

Love at Christmas and always -- Pat.

## New found poems from her journals

*Pat kept notebooks in which she wrote writing ideas; story ideas, characters, poems, etc. When she had used one she carefully crossed out the notes she had used. In her 1978 – 1986, notes (some still unused) I found three more poems. Not sure of when they were written.*

Untitled (Little prince, I can't believe...) (1981?)

Little prince, I can't believe
you came by chance,
genetic happenstance,
the first come – first served mating dance
of egg and sperm.

Your mind that reaches out and grips
your earth-deep, star-far imagining
could have belonged to nowhere else.
You could not have been different.
There is nothing accidental about you.

Untitled (There once was a man ...)      (1985?)

There once was a man
who said God
Must think it exceedingly odd
If He finds that this tree
continues to be
When there's no one about in the Quad.

Dear sir:  your astonishment's odd
I am always about in the Quad.
And that's why the tree
will continue to be.
Since observed by Yours faithfully, God.

Untitled (These weathered walls...)      (1986?)

These weathered walls,
silvery and porous as old bones,
still lie unburied.

Between the cracks
their dry voices cry
of being forsaken.

My fore-fathers left them to die
And so I stay,
and join the vigil,
listening for the sound
of iron-shod wheels.

# Poems from a 3.5" disc

Cumberland
September 20, 1992

Turning up the road that led from the river
the hearse turned again
around two sides of the house
where you were born.

One side the house,
one side the hearse,
bracketing eighty years between them.

## DALE'S CEMETERY
September 20, 1992

I wished for sunshine
so I could stroll about
this graveyard,
pointing out old stones
bearing the names of my blood relations.

Sunlight of early fall, hazy vistas,
the smell of cedars and dry, warm grass.
The smile of the gentle earth.

Like a beggar hoping for a handout,
I wanted all this
and more:
peace of mind, comfort, a sense of completion.
The meaning of it all.
All things that were never promised.

Instead we stood under umbrellas
in the pouring rain,
heels sinking into the soft earth.
Looking out past the dripping cedar boughs,
past the casket draped with carnations
and beaded with rain,
across the open fields
that might once have been farmland.

A moment of bewilderment we all shared
when the casket should have gone down
into the grave,
and didn't.
The grace of completion marred.

No sunshine, no illusions.
Only the rain,
the finality of goodbye
and the cold comfort of the stones.

## DECEMBER TWILIGHT

December 1985
April 1992

The sky, a cry of crimson
has faded to a glow
and winter for his citizens
has lit the lamp of snow.

It shines like creature under sea
or phosphorescent ghost;
or secret slow corruption
or heaven's icy host.

Such a light, so cold, so rare
sheen of sapphire, gleam of pearl
surely wells from other worlds
where griffins ride the lambent air

to prey on princely wanderers, who
pursue their quest in vain
while snow white unicorns lie unseen
upon the velvet plain.

The Mere of Dromore
July 10/93.
NB: written for a story in J's Trenchcoat IV

Dark is the oaken wood
where stands the Keep Dromore,
and dark as night the mere that lies
before its door.

I stooped beside the mere,
and who then did I see?
Fairer than any mortal queen
she beckoned me.

A cloud of midnight hair
about a face of dawn.
Eyes too bright, too perilous
to gaze upon.

And over her shoulder lay
a twist of misty tor.
A dark blue sea, a distant sail,
shipwreck on the shore.

I struck the water with my fist,
shattered the dream of dread,
and from Dromore's twice cursed mere
homeward I fled.

"Oh, why does my mother cry,
and why do my sisters weep?"

"Your brother, dearest to your heart,
lies fathoms deep."

By day I walk the shore
till darkness drives me home.
By night I shun my narrow bed
lest dreams may come.

Dreams of the fair, cruel queen
who turned my heart to stone.
Dreams of the far, enchanted land
she rules alone.

HAIKU
October 1968

Broken pewter sky
gleams to greet me at dawn
through red curtains.

Grey autumn beauty of towers
watches the green dawn
through grass blades.

INVOCATION
1962.
Titled April 6/92.

Tonight, the sky is less than pure
and winds that fly across the towers
stumble on stone, hard shod, unsure.
The darkness drowns the quiet flowers

that glow less scarlet than before
I gave my heart and mind free rein
to gallop over valley and shore
and call up shadows of lasting pain.

Small spirits I cannot rebind
rise up to haunt me, and I find
the devils that prompt me unawares
are those I wakened by my prayers.

## JANUARY TWILIGHT

January 1985
April 1992

Footprints in the snow. Wide, wolfish prints
that conjure images of savagery.
She tracked them as a child, but lost them since:
forsook the hunt for domesticity.

Here on this waste between the forest walls
wind tears white sheets across with vicious claws,
the same that strike her face. The snow that falls
begins to blur the track of giant paws.

Low to the ground, thinking themselves concealed,
the ogres crouch, their jaws agape and red.
She sees them, and turns away. For in this dusk
only the wolf is hers to love and dread.

The track lies clear... too clear, an ancient game:
the hunted has remembered how to chase.
The beast still lives, and knows her name.
He'll challenge when she meets him face to face.

## THE KILLING SEASON
November 1971
May 1992

Ten o'clock in the morning
and all the streetlights on.
The windows round are full of lights.
This is the killing season,
better to be inside.

So short a time ago
the sun stepped golden through the trees.
Now they are empty,
their fingers cold,
their glory trash.

Six months must pass
before we are warm again.

We muffle our faces
against the old enemy
who whispers, every killing season,
"One day
I will take the land back."

The Loch … July 21/93
(Revised December 1996)

Looking into the mirror
I see a country in my face.
Pale skin, pale lashes,
a tight closed mouth under a long upper lip.
Wary grey green eyes, clear but cool,
like sea water.
Ashen hair that lifts in any breeze.

The bones are closer to the skin now,
their message easier to read.
The mouth sets in its predestined manner
and the sea grey eye
glints out at me in other faces
with names like MacNeil and Shaw.

The bones and blood remember.

A stony keep, square, desolate,
jutting from the loch.
One window gleams.
Beyond, the gentle, barren hills,
green at first; beyond them,
higher and bluer hills,
layer on layer,
till at last the shoulders
of gaunt and misty tors.

This picture painted on a board at twenty.
At forty-five, a quilted panel worked.
A fantasy, I thought. A dream landscape:
heroic, enchanted.

And then at forty-seven, turning the pages
of a book, my hand paused.
Heart contracted.
Loch, keep, hills, all of it there
under my eyes.
And the captions, bringing ice to the spine:
land around Fort William,
slopes of Ben Nevis,
home of the Cameron Clan.

Looking into the mirror
of my face, and other faces,
I see my roots growing
downward and backward
through cracked stones laid up to a farmhouse door

through snow and granite and decaying fence wood,
pine choked ravines,
desolate river shores.

Back and back
past a waste of seas
to another solitude.

## THE MADILL SETTLEMENT

Feb.2/87
April 4/92

These weathered walls, silvery
and porous as old bones
lie still unburied in the wood

though year by year the forest tries
with warp of grass
and weft of mould
to weave a shroud.

Flesh to dust, wood to forest.
here, too many claims conflict.

Wind cries through glassless windows, broken doors:
"Your forefathers forsook us and we died."

Yielding the claim of blood
I join the vigil for an hour
to listen for the creak of iron shod wheels.

The Maple Grove
E.E.S. August 25, 1908 April 19, 1973

You never left us so before:
suddenly,
with no goodbye,
without a word of your return.

The masters of ceremonies tried to persuade us
you were the one lying silent
in a room heavy with flowers,
the only actor
without a speaking part.

I knew you were not there.

Others, with faces solemnly arranged
(so unlike your own)
told us you were gone
to realms
golden with angels, eternally serene.

That may be so. I don't know.
Such distant joys seem less real
than what I see
in your brothers' faces,
hear
in your children's voices:
shared looks, laughter inherited.

Perhaps you also evaded the angels,
and went to find
the home you often dreamed of:
the maple grove.

MARCH SEAS
1967
May 1992

If I could win free
like stiff seas
bursting from fetters of ice
I would do it.

If I could shatter
the distance like glass,
press months into a minute
I would do it.

But even the sea of spring
is fettered by shores.
And I have not the strength to break them,
nor the courage.

## DEXTER'S MAZE

November 1993.
For ‘The Spiral Maze’.

Ye who walk these branching ways,
warily and softly wend.
Time and chance make such a maze,
peril waits at ev'ry bend.

Here, no hope nor fear is vain.
Here, all dreams may yet come true.
Shades may live, and substance gain;
all things lost be found anew.

Yet wisely tread, or learn the cost:
that finder be forever lost.

MIGRATION
January 1964
April 6/92

Where do the birds go
when the crush of winter
plucks them from their footholds on the rocks,
when winds in November
call them off the cliffs,
sweep them in fleets out from the coast at sunset?

Remember how compact they shone
last summer:
bright brown living birds, restless and content.
Now drawn from the warm hollows
by the sea's groaning,
the sky's leaning
and the deeply grasping cold.

How do they know where to go
when night has come down,
when the waves burrow under the gale?

Where do the birds go
when they mourn off this dim coastline,
and night gathers them
and all lights blow out?

## MIRROR

July 1964 and April 1992

It seemed the house was empty.
Nobody answered her knock.
She pushed the door open and heard no sound
but the tick of a dusty clock.

She climbed the stairs to look
and found no one at all.
Only the ghosts and the furniture
and a mirror on the wall.

Who is that in the mirror?
Surely nobody she knows.
Not her thin, sick, pallid self
in a blouse of ashy rose.

Hair billows, whispers, shines
about a blossom face.
Hands detain the vagrant curls
with semaphoric grace.

Eyes that glow like moonstones
far more alive than she.
A smile compact of morning,
too bright for sympathy.

And over the slender shoulder
a twist of misty tor.
A dark blue sea, a distant sail,
a horseman on the shore.

She strikes the mirror with her fist,
shatters the cruel glass.
She leaves the room with its dust and blood
by the only door left to pass.

She walks the noisy streets of town
till darkness drives her home.
And then lies rigid in her bed
dreading the dreams to come.

Dreams of the far heroic lands
denied to such as she.
Dreams of the swinging crystal shoals,
the kingdoms by the sea.

## NOVEMBER

November 28, 1984

April 4, 1992

October past, like vital middle age,
quicker than fear or expectation gone,
November storms upon us, lean and wan,
all silvered, like King Lear upon the stage.
It's growing old that sets him in a rage:
the grave indignity of being bundled on
before his business properly is done;
they snatched the book before he'd filled the page.

November's tears, like stones against the glass
bite bitterer than summer's velvet rain.
The green blood bleaches from the tattered hill,
the red from wrinkled cheek. He dreads the pass
to icy sleep. Then takes up hope again,
recalls the Resurrection, and is still.

RONDEAU
Dec. 1964
April 1992

Do you wish to dam tight
this fast running river
and cage up forever
blue herons in flight?

A fool with a fool's sight
would linger forever.
Would you cage herons white
and hold back the swift river?

Time has his own might.
His fatal gifts never
return to the giver.
Would you cage herons tight?

Have you seen them in flight?

## SEEING OCTOBER
April 1992

Dance of leaves on cobalt sky,
flare and startle of cardinal's wing:
these I store against the day I die.

Nets of gold in the afternoon:
crimson darting in mid-air,
embers underfoot, glowing in the gloom.

Sunset flush on red brick wall,
windows winking like spectacles.
Beneath the eyes of stars, blue evenfall.

Deep the dark, my candle dead:
midnight's breath will blow me blind.
Then all I stored today will light my mind
till morning breaks ahead.

## TWILIGHT OF THE YEAR

October 1975
May 1992.

End of a stony afternoon
bitten off and swallowed by November.
The elms have an ancient, deaf and brittle look,
windless,
their tangles too embraided
to be stirred.

Light gathers.
Colour bleeds upward into the west.
Dark gathers,
thickens like smoke in the streets.
Night pursues
and streetlights leap like moons out of the air.

Across the street visitors ring,
and the drowsy house
opens a golden eye.

## VOYAGE

1963
Titled April 6/92

Smooth blue canals and seas
bounding banks feathered
Dark hearted clouds in fleets
ragged and weathered

Last dregs of solid mist
edged round with lightning
sail on like pirate ships,
straight to the brightening.

The round sun's radiant face:
quicksilver burning.
White dazzle of his rim
segmented, ferning,

curling up wisps of light
from the sun centre
stiff curve. From summertime
drops to his winter.

www.ingramcontent.com/pod-product-compliance
Ingram Content Group UK Ltd.
Pitfield, Milton Keynes, MK11 3LW, UK
UKHW041904190726
13854UKWH00003B/1081